ENGLAND

THE NATURE OF THE LAND

Photographs of National Nature Reserves in England

ENGLISH
NATURE

First published in Great Britain in 1999 by
Colin Baxter Photography Ltd.
Grantown-on-Spey
Moray PH26 3NA

Text and Map Copyright © English Nature 1999
Photographs Copyright © Graham Nobles 1999
All rights reserved

A CIP catalogue record for this book is available from the British Library

ISBN 1-84107-002-5

Printed in Hong Kong

Front Cover Photographs:
(TL): Whitbarrow, Cumbria (TR): Stiperstones, Shropshire
(BL): Cotswold Commons and Beechwoods, Gloucestershire (BR): The Lizard, Cornwall
Back Cover Photograph: East Dartmoor Woods and Heaths, Devon
Page One Photograph: Dwarf Thistle, Ebbor Gorge, Somerset
Page Four Photograph: Moor House – Upper Teesdale, Cumbria and County Durham

ENGLAND

THE NATURE OF THE LAND

Photographs of National Nature Reserves in England

PHOTOGRAPHS BY GRAHAM NOBLES

FOREWORD BY BARONESS YOUNG OF OLD SCONE

INTRODUCTION BY ALEX KIRBY

Colin Baxter Photography, Grantown-on-Spey, Scotland

CONTENTS

MOCCAS PARK, HEREFORD AND WORCESTER

Moccas Park, or Moccas Deer Park as it is also known, dates from
the seventeenth century and is one of the largest and most diverse examples of wood
pasture surviving in Britain. The ancient parkland oak, beech and sweet chestnut trees make
Moccas Park one of the most important sites for deadwood invertebrates in England.

FOREWORD

SOME OF THE most important nature reserves in England are also the most unknown. The National Nature Reserves, of which there are around two hundred countrywide, are stunning areas for conservation and biodiversity and they belong to all of us. Apart from their importance for conserving special, rare and threatened species and habitats of England, they also provide opportunities for the public to experience the thrilling facets of nature at first hand.

The NNR series, some managed by English Nature and some by key partners, also act as a test bed for techniques of conservation management and provide sites for conservation research of many kinds.

But most of all they are just very special places and it is this specialness which this book celebrates, marking the fiftieth anniversary of the legislation which established the concept of National Nature Reserves. I hope you enjoy these glorious portraits of fifty of our NNRs and give in to the inevitable urge to experience them first hand.

Barbara Young

Baroness Young of Old Scone
Chairman, English Nature

THE NATURE OF THE LAND

ONE BRIGHT WINTER'S day, I decided to take the dog on a different route for his Saturday morning walk. Just beyond a nearby village we found a muddy track I'd never seen before. We headed uphill away from the road, and followed the track between high hedges until it came out on the short turf of the South Downs. He and I had the morning to ourselves, apart from the sheep, and the skylarks, and the occasional distant rumble of an aircraft climbing out to head over the English Channel to some far horizon.

It was brisk up there, with an east wind, so we didn't dawdle. In half an hour or so the track brought us across the downland to a stile, beside which stood a discreet green notice, proclaiming the land across the fence a National Nature Reserve. It was the site of an Iron Age fort, the ramparts and ditches undisturbed for generations, and home now to a wealth of rare plants and insects.

We pressed on towards the summit, revelling in the sunlit emptiness, the dog rolling over and over on the grass in sheer delight with the world. And as we reached the top, all at once it hit me – a wall of sound, a constant steady drumming, low but insistent, driving the skylarks' song beyond recall.

There, at the foot of the hill where we stood, ran the main south-coast road, pell-mell with urgent travellers, rumbling with heavy goods vehicles. Every now and then a train clattered along the line that keeps the highway company. The real world pressed close.

After a few minutes, we turned back. A few yards downhill, and the silence was once again almost complete, with only the lark song and the distant sheep to remind us we were not alone on those bare hills.

I'd always thought until then that nature reserves were a generally good idea, something to be glad that someone else had thought of and bothered to create and protect. But I came down the track seeing them in a sharper, more focused light – a vivid reminder of what we still have that's worth preserving, and of the pressures that could mean we lose even more of it.

Preservation? Is that the sum total of what our National Nature Reserves are for? There's all too often a whiff of defensiveness, retreat even, about the idea of preservation. If that is what the reserves are about, then perhaps it might be better to let them go, to allow the onward march of progress – or whatever you want to call it – to bulldoze them, concrete them over, turn them into car parks, or theme parks, or anything that marks them out as part of the human domain.

One of the architects of the modern network of nature reserves we have today is Max Nicholson, the former director of the Nature Conservancy (the Conservancy was the early post-war ancestor of English Nature, and of its Welsh and Scottish colleagues. The story of why we now have three bodies where once there was one belongs elsewhere.)

Max Nicholson wrote a book which explains the genesis of the movement that led to the creation of the reserves, and its rationale (*Britain's Nature Reserves*, Country Life Limited, 1957). It lists all the reserves then in existence throughout Britain (the Conservancy was not responsible for Northern Ireland).

Reading the Introduction, I was brought up short to find the author describing reserves as 'outdoor living museums or wildernesses in which nature can be preserved as a national

HICKLING BROAD, NORFOLK.

heritage'. Wildlife in aspic, then?

Museums do not rate very highly with many people in millennial Britain. That is partly, I suppose, because so many of them now charge for admission. But it may also have something to do with the age of the shrinking attention span, the concentration on the present and its opportunities for gratification, or at least fulfilment.

But museums remain as important as they have ever been. 'Those who cannot remember the past are condemned to repeat it', wrote George Santayana in 1905. And perhaps those who today cannot even glimpse the past are condemned to lose it. A single nature reserve, let alone a whole network of them, must be worthwhile if it opens the eyes of new generations to what their forebears enjoyed. It has nothing to do with aspic, everything to do with vision. The Antarctic hero Scott wrote to his wife about their son, in his last letter: 'Make the boy interested in natural history if you can; it is better than games'. She did, and Peter Scott repaid her efforts a thousandfold, with results for which we remain thankful today. What chance of finding and inspiring the Peter Scotts of the next century if the natural places are all gone?

Some, at least, then, of Max Nicholson's vision lives on. But can we still speak forty years later, as he did, of 'wildernesses'? It's certainly stretching language to do so in most of south-east England, domesticated, manicured and parcelled out to the last hectare.

One of the most notable achievements of him and his generation, though, has been to hand on to us an entire system of truly national nature reserves. They stretch, in England, from the Solway Firth to Canterbury, from Lindisfarne to The Lizard. There are very few counties without a single reserve to their name, though as you would expect the parts of the country that used to earn their keep from heavy industry have fewer than rural England. But wilderness of some sort is still there, if that is what you want.

The reserves we have today are intended to be important not only in their own right, but as representative of something worth cherishing because of its wider significance. Meeting this double criterion means that they are a mosaic of very different places, and sizes, in widely differing locations. Some are remote from the big cities, some almost on their doorsteps. But all of them have one feature in common: they are a national treasure, and a national responsibility.

English Nature, the body responsible for designating and looking after England's National Nature Reserves (and for putting up the discreet notice I saw by the stile), offers a definition of what the reserves are for. It starts by saying they were 'established to protect the most important areas of wildlife habitat and geological formations in Britain…'.

So far, so good. But English Nature, I am fairly sure, would not see itself as primarily the curator of a series of outdoor museums. And if you and I choose to see the reserves at least partly in that light, a window onto a largely lost world, English Nature has a much wider concept of what they are for.

There are in any case several problems with the reserves-as-museums approach. The first is the obvious fact that the reserves show us not a snapshot of England preserved from time immemorial, but of what things were like just a few generations ago. The land has been worked so long, and so intensively, that what the reserves can show us now dates from a recent past, not from some supposed Arcadian golden age.

Another and more basic problem with seeing the reserves primarily as museums is that they are simply too valuable for that, important as it is. Besides being a record of the past, they are a resource for the present. And that definition by English Nature explains how: it goes on to say that they are protected as 'places for scientific research'.

WOODWALTON FEN, CAMBRIDGESHIRE
The fen lies at the lowest and most westerly part of the East
Anglian fens and is one of England's oldest nature reserves. The reserve is well
known for its different plants and invertebrates associated with wet fen.

MARTIN DOWN, HAMPSHIRE

An extensive chalk grassland plain bordered by massive linear prehistoric earthworks, the whole area being rich in archaeological features from the Bronze Age to more recent times. The ancient grassland is rich in plants and butterflies.

So forget museums for a moment, and think of laboratories, because that is what the reserves are, every one of them. They earn their way onto the select list of National Nature Reserves by virtue of their ability to extend our knowledge and understanding of the natural world.

In some cases that means they are laboratories for applied environmental science – workshops where techniques of protection and of improvement can be tried and then shared.

Thirty years ago, English Nature says, the reserves tended often to be isolated places. Today, though, they may well form part of a local network of habitat management. And they are also 'centres of expertise, which demonstrate to landowners, local authorities, conservation workers and others the techniques of planning, habitat management and environmental monitoring. Increasingly, the reserves and their managers form part of a broader programme to conserve wildlife and scenery…'.

One example of this collaborative approach is in the West of England, where English Nature, Somerset County Council, the Royal Society for the Protection of Birds and the Somerset Trust for Nature Conservation are all involved in the Avalon Marshes project, flooding old peat cuttings on and around the Shapwick Heath reserve. Good for them: looking after natural England is too complex and urgent for anyone to try to go it alone. There are quite enough prima donnas trying to leave their mark on the environment already.

Hands-on, dirty boots experience of what works is immensely valuable. But it is probably that reference to the reserves' value as places for environmental monitoring which is most crucial to understanding why they exist. They are, after all, sites which have earned their place in the pantheon by virtue of their value to science.

English Nature writes: 'Long-term monitoring, whether of species or of broader environment change, is today the most important scientific function of National Nature Reserves. They provide relatively undisturbed places where, for example, the effects of "acid rain" can be monitored, or where ecologists can learn about the natural development of woodland. Many of our reserve managers contribute to national monitoring schemes, such as the Wetland Bird Survey or the Butterfly Transect Scheme'.

Change to the natural world now is rapid and unpredictable. We can make what predictions we like about, say, climate change, but we cannot confidently write in the consequences of what is called 'positive feedback' – the possibility that something we *can* foresee will become a new factor in the equation and itself contribute to results we cannot predict. Laboratories are likely to prove even more vital than museums.

National Nature Reserves were first mooted in 1949, under the National Parks and Access to the Countryside Act. Two years later, the first was established, in north-west Scotland. And in 1952 the six first English reserves were designated: Yarner Wood in Devon, Ham Street Woods in Kent, Cavenham Heath in Suffolk, Kingley Vale in Sussex, Holme Fen in Cambridgeshire, and Moor House in Cumbria.

Nowadays English Nature still operates under the same 1949 Act of Parliament in discharging its statutory duty to protect the best of our wildlife by designating a site as a reserve. It takes a number of factors into account in doing so – the fragility of and the threat to habitats and species, for example, the size of the site (it prefers them to be as large as possible), the lack of disturbance, the presence of communities rich in species, particularly rare ones, and what it calls 'the degree of "naturalness" of the site', which presumably means that if the new Jubilee tube line through east London uncovers some rare geology, it won't stand much chance of being declared a reserve.

Today's world is very different from 1952's. We still rightly recognise and give thanks for the vision which inspired Max Nicholson and his peers in setting up the reserve network. But that vision has developed as the world has changed. Fifty years ago, very few of us would have even heard of acid rain or climate change, let alone known what they were, or what significance they would have acquired by the end of the century. We need the reserves even more than we did then, and for reasons we could not have guessed at.

One change, relatively unimportant in itself, but an eloquent commentary on a changing society, is the role today of English Nature compared with its predecessor five decades ago. In the 1950s it was regarded as axiomatic that the body which designated National Nature Reserves would in almost every case also own and run them. Today that is no longer so, and English Nature is the outright owner of fewer than a quarter of all the reserves, though it does own parts of many others. Nearly half the total area designated as reserves is in fact leased: much of it is inter-tidal land owned by the Crown, and leased by English Nature from the Crown Estate Commissioners. Much of the rest of the reserve land remains in private hands but is managed, either directly by English Nature or in partnership with the owners. And a small part is owned and managed by what is called 'an Approved Body'.

Approved Bodies sound very official. In practice they are groups with aims and expertise that mirror English Nature's – charities, companies or institutions whose land is nationally important to nature conservation and also managed to very high standards. With the owners' agreement, and once it is satisfied that both the site itself and the owners' management standards meet its own, English Nature can then declare the site a National Nature Reserve. The category covers groups like county wildlife trusts, local authorities, the National Trust, the RSPB and the City of London Corporation. Because the declaration of land owned by an Approved Body is made under a different law (Section 35 of the Wildlife and Countryside Act 1981), these reserves are sometimes known simply as Section 35 sites.

It may seem a small point to be bothered about who owns and runs a reserve, given that the end result is the same. But over the last twenty years public ownership has become a derided concept, and privatisation is touted as the panacea for virtually every social ill. So I am glad of a body like English Nature that is pragmatic enough to recognise that one approach will work in some cases, another elsewhere. Horses for courses, perhaps? It gets the right results, anyway.

I cherish my local reserve (and I don't think it odd that I regard a *national* reserve as both mine and local – that's the sort of effect they can have on you). But I don't imagine that it comprehends in one tiny area (49 hectares) the wealth of species and habitats that we can all call our own. Apart from the chalk downland I find there, I can go to some of the other reserves up and down England and find salt marshes, sand dunes, meadows, heaths, woodlands and moors. There are estuaries and fens, bogs and upland pastures. I can, if I hunt around, find the homes of Adonis blue butterflies, fritillary lilies, dragonflies and dormice, though there's no guarantee that I shall actually see them. I might not even know that I have a chance of seeing them, because the prudent people at English Nature say they 'do not always advertise rarities, for fear of attracting too much attention to them'. You have been warned – or not. There is even one marine nature reserve, Lundy Island off the North Devon coast, and there are hopes that before long there will be others.

But it will certainly be unusual if you cannot visit a reserve, or at least part of it. You and I are welcome at most reserves, though there may be parts where we cannot go, for fear of disrupting the

KIELDERHEAD, NORTHUMBERLAND

A large expanse of undisturbed upland moorland on the edge of Kielder Forest,
the largest planted forest in Europe. The reserve contains a complex of dry and wet
heath and acid grasslands, and an important community of upland breeding birds.

MOOR HOUSE – UPPER TEESDALE, CUMBRIA AND COUNTY DURHAM
A high upland reserve that contains large areas of characteristic North Pennine
moorland and valley grasslands grazed by sheep and cattle, and also flower-rich hay meadows.

scientific work which remains their *raison d'être*. Visitors are asked to respect the Country Code, and activities like lighting fires, camping, and using metal detectors are frowned on, reasonably enough. In some cases, also quite reasonably, dogs are frowned on, though this may take some explaining to your companion.

English Nature wanted to find out what visitors to the reserves thought about the excursion they'd just made. So it ran a survey, stretching over three years, at fifteen sites. This found – as surveys of this sort often do – that four out of five visitors were 'completely satisfied or very pleased' with their experience. No surprises there, then. But the survey also found large numbers of people saying they wanted to be given more information about the reserve they were visiting. As only two-thirds of those surveyed had even heard of English Nature, it sounds as if we could do with rather more of those discreet dark green notices, telling us what we are about to see and who we have to thank for it.

The National Nature Reserves are often called the jewels in England's crown, the sites which cry out for special protection because of the wealth they harbour. But it would be wrong to think of sleuths from English Nature haphazardly roaming the country in the hope of discovering some hitherto neglected treasure which they can then designate. The process is far more methodical than that, and it is influenced by several other policies which are among English Nature's priorities.

One of these is the identification and description of Natural Areas. English Nature has published profiles of the 120 Natural Areas it has identified, each containing a description of the Area's nature conservation interest, and of the impacts and trends which are affecting it. The scheme covers the entire land surface, including the coast of England, and work has begun on describing six marine Natural Areas as well.

What this means is that English Nature now has a more accurate yardstick to help it to decide whether it ought to declare or acquire new reserves. If it finds that one possible candidate for designation represents a type of habitat already well represented by reserves in similar Natural Areas, for instance, it can decide to concentrate its efforts elsewhere on rescuing a site with a habitat that is under-represented.

Another policy that affects the national reserves is the UK Biodiversity Action Plan (or BAP, in the jargon), which English Nature calls 'the key national initiative that drives our strategy'. This has identified the most important threatened species and habitats, and is developing plans to halt and reverse their declines. Closely linked to it is the Species Recovery Programme, which is working to help eighty different sorts of flora and fauna. Thirty of those threatened plants and animals have already met the initial objectives for their recovery. Also of importance are the European habitats and species directives which have resulted in the Natura 2000 sites, which in England includes many National Nature Reserves.

Taken together, BAP with the Species Recovery Programme and Natura 2000 provide English Nature with a much more clearly focused instrument for deciding where to direct its efforts, a way of ensuring, for example, that we do not get a plague of dormice while ignoring the tenuous hold on survival of the natterjack toad. Together with the Natural Areas approach, it adds up to a more coherent way of deciding what to seek to conserve, and in what order of priority.

Museums, laboratories – and what else? The National Nature Reserves are surely zoos, in the way that they serve as cradles for the recovery of threatened species. Or perhaps a zoo is a less apt metaphor than an ark, a place of refuge where wild creatures can recuperate and find safety until conditions outside are again favourable for them to thrive. It is a sign of how far we have come, and how much we have lost, that we need to think in terms of an ark at all. But with the extinction of species as familiar as the sky-lark predicted before today's children have grown to maturity, an ark it will have to be if there is to be any hope of recovery.

The National Nature Reserves, *all of them together*, amount to not much more than half of one per cent of the surface of England. There are around 200 of them, totalling just under 80,000 hectares (there are probably nearly ten times as many nature reserves of all descriptions, but it is only the national ones for which English Nature is responsible). Is that enough? Not remotely. But what prospect is there of extending them significantly?

As always, it is partly a question of money. It doesn't cost much per head: each of us pays around five pence a year for English Nature's reserves. But it does not have limitless cash for managing or leasing them – or, as a last resort, for buying them outright.

There is better news, though. Early in 1999 English Nature contributed £50,000 towards the cost of buying the Dingle Marshes, a valuable site on the Suffolk coast which will become part of Walberswick NNR in due course, and which is home to bitterns, avocets and water voles – and to much else besides. The Marshes cost far more than that, though, and £559,000 came in the form of a grant from the Heritage Lottery Fund to the RSPB and the Suffolk Wildlife Trust.

That contribution from the Fund was the latest instalment of a series of donations totalling £35 million over four years. With that sort of money – whether it goes to voluntary or statutory groups – it is possible to talk seriously of enlarging the family of National Nature Reserves.

Help from the Fund, and from the Government, can therefore make the difference between survival and extinction for those species which have no hope at all in the hostile world outside the reserves. There will still be problems – the risk of a chain of reserves isolated in a largely sterile landscape, for instance, and the temptation to designate sites which do not really measure up to the exacting standards required of a national reserve, simply for the sake of safeguarding a species or habitat which would otherwise go to the wall. Despite the risks, though, I hope that English Nature will lead the way in expanding the present set of reserves. Only that will keep us in touch with our past, help us to understand the present, and give us hope for the future.

In *England's National Nature Reserves* (T & A D Poyser, 1994), Peter Marren writes:

> 'Nature reserves are still our best guarantee that rare wild animals and plants can find a refuge, and that the richest parts of our natural heritage will be passed on intact to generations yet unborn. In their various guises – sanctuaries, outdoor museums and laboratories, test-beds for management techniques or simply as places to see wild plants and animals – National Nature Reserves have served England well these past forty years. We had the advantage of an early start and the work of three centuries of English naturalists on which to draw… England's National Nature Reserves may not boast the most dramatic scenery on the planet, but they do form a unique and wonderful record of how man and nature can still live together on a crowded island'.

Go to your nearest reserve, or go again, or go to one you've never been to before. Above all, the National Nature Reserves are places of *hope*.

Alex Kirby

PEWSEY DOWNS, WILTSHIRE.

CHAPTER ONE

THE NORTH-EAST

THE NORTH-EAST is traditionally associated with coal, ship-building, iron and steel and heavy industry as well as a strong sense of community. But it has other faces. There are the wild uplands and the rugged coast as well as the sense of the historic and the spiritual embodied in such places as Lindisfarne and Durham.

The North Pennines form a distinct block, characterised by high heather moorland, to the west of the region. Cross Fell is the highest point in the Pennine chain. The Whin Sill, a volcanic rock exposure, forms dramatic features such as High Force, the largest waterfall in England.

In Northumberland, tracks of rolling heather and grass moorland cover the higher ground of the Cheviots and the border moors. Farming is mostly upland pastoral, with game management becoming increasingly important at higher altitudes. Native woodland is scarce, but Kielder Forest lies brooding to the south-west.

The coast of Northumberland is diverse, high sandstone cliffs near Berwick and low-lying limestone ones at Bamburgh. At Lindisfarne, cut off from the mainland at high tide, the inter-tidal areas are internationally important for wintering waterfowl. When the tide is in, the island's special atmosphere will help you understand its historic spiritual significance. Out to sea, the Farne Islands provide a home for large numbers of seabirds.

LINDISFARNE, NORTHUMBERLAND (OPPOSITE). INGLEBOROUGH, SOUTHERNSCALES, NORTH YORKSHIRE (ABOVE).

KIELDERHEAD, NORTHUMBERLAND

An upland stream flowing through acidic grass and heather moorland. Elsewhere on the reserve occur wet bog communities dominated by bog mosses, and flushes dominated by sedges and moisture-demanding flowering plants.

KIELDERHEAD, NORTHUMBERLAND

This large expanse of high moorland is dissected by a number of valleys. Management in the past was predominantly either as sheep grazing, or as grouse moor with intensive heather burning and predator control. Much of the moor has not been grazed or burnt for forty years, however, and the reserve provides a very important contrast to those moorlands that are still managed in this way.

GREENLEE LOUGH, NORTHUMBERLAND

Close by Hadrian's Wall, Greenlee Lough is a shallow upland lough (lake)
containing important submerged aquatic plants and fringed with reeds and rushes. Wet birch
and willow carr (fen scrub), and bog communities also occur around the lough, and the reserve
is used extensively in winter by wildfowl such as whooper swans, bean geese and wigeon.

MOOR HOUSE – UPPER TEESDALE, CUMBRIA AND COUNTY DURHAM

The important wildlife features of this internationally famous reserve include a unique rich arctic-alpine flora associated with the very rare sugar limestone grassland of Upper Teesdale, and strong populations of moorland breeding birds.

MOOR HOUSE – UPPER TEESDALE, CUMBRIA AND COUNTY DURHAM

Fast-flowing high moorland streams, though relatively low in their variety of plant and
animal species, contain important communities and species which have adapted to this harsh environment.

RIVER TEES, MOOR HOUSE – UPPER TEESDALE, CUMBRIA AND COUNTY DURHAM

The North Pennines, of which the reserve is part, is one of the most remote areas of England.
Many of the visitors to the reserve are walkers along the Pennine Way seeking a 'wilderness experience'.

CLOCKWISE FROM TOP LEFT: EIDER DUCK, SHAG, PUFFIN AND SHAG
Up to twenty-one species of seabirds nest on the Farne Islands.

FARNE ISLANDS, NORTHUMBERLAND

This archipelago of islands off the coast of Northumberland, which is
important for breeding puffins and other seabirds, holds the largest grey seal
population on the east coast of England, and has important marine wildlife.

LINDISFARNE, NORTHUMBERLAND

Areas of shingle and rocky shore provide suitable conditions for seaweeds and a specialised invertebrate fauna associated with them, and whelks and periwinkles. These in turn provide important feeding opportunities for birds such as the purple sandpiper and rock pipit, and also a suitable breeding habitat for terns and waders.

LINDISFARNE, NORTHUMBERLAND

A dynamic coastal reserve undergoing physiographic changes, some of which may be of a cyclical nature.
A full range of coastal vegetation is found on the reserve, which has been relatively undisturbed by human practices.

MALHAM TARN, NORTH YORKSHIRE

Windswept trees by an upland lake in the Craven Limestone district of North Yorkshire (above).
Malham Tarn is the highest elevation marl lake in Britain. It is rich in submerged plants, and is bordered by wetland
plant communities ranging from rich fen to acid mire in a combination found nowhere else in Britain (opposite).

INGLEBOROUGH, NORTH YORKSHIRE

Ingleborough contains possibly the finest suite of surface and carst landforms to be found within any small area in Britain. The glaciated plateau of the reserve contains a wide range of landform features, ranging from the classic limestone pavement (as illustrated) and bare scars to dry valleys and gorges, blind valleys, sinkholes, shakeholes and collapse features. Limestone pavement is an internationally rare landform.

INGLEBOROUGH, NORTH YORKSHIRE

Grykes protect plants, such as the rare bird's eye primrose,
from being grazed by sheep. They also allow a dwarf-type scrub
community to develop in an otherwise treeless environment.

DUNCOMBE PARK, NORTH YORKSHIRE

Gnarled and ancient trees, set in Grade I listed parkland, contain
rot holes and hollow trunks that provide the habitat for rare and spectacular
insects. The Park contains fifteen listed buildings of historical interest.

TEESMOUTH, CLEVELAND

Wildlife coexists with its industrial neighbours through co-operation
and agreed management at this reserve which protects the core feeding and roosting
sites for internationally important wader and wildfowl populations.

SPURN, HUMBERSIDE

This three-and-a-half-mile sand peninsula (above) in the mouth of the Humber Estuary is of great
importance to migratory and wintering birds. It is a dynamic peninsula that was created by natural coastal processes
and continues to be altered by them. Attempts to stabilise the peninsula have interrupted these natural processes, but
all involved with the reserve are looking for ways to allow the natural processes to continue (opposite).

CHAPTER TWO

THE NORTH-WEST

FROM THE GENTLE landscape of Cheshire, through the industrial belt of Greater Manchester, Merseyside and south Lancashire, to the grandeur of the Lake District, the North-West shows many faces.

Cheshire's lush rolling plain is dominated by intensive dairy farming, or by beef and arable production. Its meres and mosses are wetlands of international importance. Urban development and industry rule the Mersey Basin. However its coastline is important, the dunes of the Sefton coast providing significant wildlife habitats.

Intensive farming typifies the Lancashire plain, yet despite this, rare plant species such as the purple ramping fumitory still occur. The estuaries of the rivers Ribble, Lune and Wyre support huge flocks of migratory wildfowl and wading birds, which also feed and roost on the farmland along the coastal plain.

Undoubtedly, the most dramatic countryside is found in the Lake District, with all its poetic inspiration. In the north and centre are the spectacular high fells and heather moors. In the south, the low fells display their gentle, rolling, rocky and densely wooded character. But throughout, it is the lakes themselves, from the large and familiar, like Windermere or Coniston, to the small secluded tarns, that give the area its special beauty.

WHITBARROW, CUMBRIA (OPPOSITE). RED SQUIRREL, AINSDALE SAND DUNES, LANCASHIRE (ABOVE).

BASSENTHWAITE LAKE, CUMBRIA

Grazing meadows slope down to the lake shore with a backdrop
of the steeply rising hillsides and screes of Skiddaw. The reserve is the
fourth-largest lake in the Lake District, but one of the shallowest.

BASSENTHWAITE LAKE, CUMBRIA

Bassenthwaite Lake is the home of the vendace, a rare fish that occurs in only one other site in Britain.
The lake has a rich aquatic flora, and also has important populations of breeding and wintering birds.

SMARDALE GILL, CUMBRIA

The cuttings and embankments of the disused Darlington to Tebay railway line are part of
this reserve, which is of particular importance for its population of the Scotch Argus butterfly.

SMARDALE GILL, CUMBRIA

Steeply sloping limestone grassland
and ancient ash woodland make up this
reserve. The grassland contains a rich
variety of plants that includes the scarce
bird's eye primrose and blue moor grass,
and other notable species such as alpine
bistort, and greater butterfly and fragrant
orchids. The ancient woodland ground
flora includes bird's nest orchid, herb
paris and common wintergreen. Red
squirrels occur on the reserve, and the
breeding birds include redstart, wood
warbler and pied flycatcher.

ROUDSEA WOOD AND MOSSES, CUMBRIA

The reserve consists of an exceptionally diverse range of habitats, ranging from estuary and salt marsh, through woodland on both slate and limestone, to an estuarine raised mire complex of mosses. The woodland covers two ridges separated by a shallow valley that contains a valley mire and small tarn. The east ridge carries an ash-oak wood with some small-leaved lime, gean and birch. The west ridge carries a contrasting sessile oak wood with some birch, rowan and hazel.

ROSTHERNE MERE, CHESHIRE

The deepest (98 ft/30 m) and largest of the Cheshire meres, which rarely
freezes over even in hard winters, is an important site for wintering wildfowl. The
associated reedbeds, woodlands and grasslands increase the variety of wildlife found on
the reserve. The reserve has been a focus for freshwater research since the early 1900s.

GREAT ASBY SCAR, CUMBRIA

Harsh upland conditions, but also over-grazing by sheep in the past, have
produced a wild, open landscape where limestone pavement lies amongst a mosaic of
calcareous and acidic grasslands, heathland and bracken. Extraction of the weather-worn
limestone from the pavement for use as rockery stone has resulted in severe damage.

GREAT ASBY SCAR, CUMBRIA
The grykes (fissures) in the limestone pavement provide sheltered and humid conditions
similar to that in woodlands, a niche that many plants typical of woodlands take advantage of.

WHITBARROW, CUMBRIA

Blue moor-grass grassland is characteristic of the upland limestones of northern England. Rarer plants – eg hoary rockrose, dark red helleborine, and bird's foot sedge – are associated with the reserve's thin soils of cliff tops and limestone pavements.

WHITBARROW, CUMBRIA

All but the very largest of England's NNRs are part of and affected by the wider
landscape within which they sit. For the smaller reserves in the south, within a landscape heavily
affected by modern agriculture, the impact can sometimes be deleterious. But at reserves such as
Whitbarrow, the continuity of wildlife-rich habitat beyond the reserve enhances its value.

WHITBARROW, CUMBRIA

Southwards the reserve overlooks the Cumbrian coast (above).
Birch and ash woodland is spreading into the reserve where sheep
grazing is not as heavy as it once was (opposite).

CHAPTER THREE

THE MIDLANDS

THE MIDLANDS contain a wide variety of landscapes, including the Shropshire Hills and the lowlands of Hereford in the west; the rugged splendour of the Peak District and the history and legend of Sherwood and Rockingham Forests; and the flat fertile plains of Lincolnshire and the wide expanse of The Wash in the east.

Hereford is mainly lowland in character with some isolated hills and a rolling plateau in the north-east. Agriculture includes arable, pasture, hopfields and orchards. Further north there are the characteristic 'hogs' backs' of the Shropshire Hills. Here is the distinctive wild and exposed ridge of Stiperstones; and the broad upland plateau of the Long Mynd can seem like another world.

The Peak District with its hills and dales is beloved by walkers and climbers and ancient woodland can be visited in places like Sherwood and Rockingham.

Further east are the uplands of the Lincolnshire Wolds, characterised by large fields bordered by neatly trimmed hawthorn hedges. The Wolds fall away to the coastal plain edged with large tracts of salt marsh, sand dunes and tidal mud flats, much of which is now protected. Close by lies The Wash, an internationally important ecosystem, home to huge numbers of migrating wildfowl.

DERBYSHIRE DALES (OPPOSITE). QUARTZITE TORS, STIPERSTONES, SHROPSHIRE (ABOVE).

DOWNTON GORGE, HEREFORD AND WORCESTER

Downton Gorge, of which the reserve is part, was formed by the River Teme cutting down through a ridge of limestone, siltstones and sandstones. Rock exposures have yielded rare fossil remains of primitive fish, and a well-preserved fossil fauna is evident at many locations. The woodland is a mixture of sessile oak, ash, lime, wych elm and birch with rich flower and high plant communities. Otters and polecats are found on the reserve, and buzzards are a common sight as they quarter the woods and meadows for prey.

BARDNEY LIMEWOODS, LINCOLNSHIRE

Patterns of colour and texture, bark and moss, characteristic of old trees. Britain's greatest concentration of
woodlands dominated by small-leaved lime occurs in the Bardney Forest, famous for its varied butterfly populations.

GIBRALTAR POINT, LINCOLNSHIRE

Built by complex coastal processes at the entrance of the huge Wash estuary, the intertidal mud flats, salt marsh and sand dunes of the reserve are a haven for migrating and wintering birds. A field-study station and an information centre explain the importance of the site to the many thousand annual visitors. Shingle and sand provide suitable conditions for nesting waders and terns, and habitats for plants adapted to withstand a salty environment (opposite and above).

FENN'S, WHIXALL AND BETTISFIELD MOSSES, SHROPSHIRE

A black-faced darter, one of many dragonflies, damsel flies and other insects found on
Fenn's, Whixhall and Bettisfield Mosses. An intensive rehabilitation programme of tree and scrub
clearance, and raising water levels by damming is underway on the reserve, following the near
destruction of the site by intensive commercial peat extraction before it became an NNR.

FENN'S, WHIXALL AND BETTISFIELD MOSSES, SHROPSHIRE

Maintenance of a high water table is essential to rehabilitate and then maintain the specialised wildlife importance of these lowland raised mires. Mire species are rapidly recolonising rehabilitated areas. This success story is being proactively demonstrated to other peatland managers, and is used to promote the value of peatlands for wildlife. The mire species include carnivorous plants, lesser bladderwort, and great and oblong-leaved sundews associated with nutrient-poor peatlands.

DERBYSHIRE DALES

The contrasting vegetation of North Derbyshire's south-facing slopes are well demonstrated in Lathkill Dale, particularly amongst the grassland communities. On the warmer and drier south-facing slopes, the grasslands are particularly flower-rich and are characterised by low-growing species such as rock-rose, salad burnet and wild thyme. The cooler and moister north-facing slopes are less flower-rich and are characterised by taller species such as meadowsweet, common valerian and burnet saxifrage.

DERBYSHIRE DALES

Steep-sided valleys cut into the White Peak carboniferous
limestone plateau. The White Peak is one of the most important masses
of carboniferous limestone in Britain, and is of geological importance.

DERBYSHIRE DALES

The woodlands of the reserve are dominated by ash, but in those regarded as the oldest, wych elm
and small-leaved lime are also present. The ground flora has a very wide range of rare and common plants.
In moist areas, ferns, mosses and liverworts form a central component of the reserve's importance.

64

DERBYSHIRE DALES

A pyramidal orchid, characteristic of
lime-rich soils found in these limestone
dales. Sensitive management is required
to maintain the right grassland structures
required for the wide range of plants
and animals (particularly insects and
other invertebrates) associated with the
grasslands. This is achieved by controlled
grazing managed by local farmers to
produce a mosaic of sward heights at
different times during the year, but
favouring light grazing in summer to
allow plentiful flowering and seeding.

AQUALATE MERE, STAFFORDSHIRE

The reserve is the largest of the nationally important meres and mosses in the North-West Midlands. A number of streams feed into the mere from surrounding pasture fields. Woodland fringes the mere in places, and extensive reedswamp, alder and willow carr, damp grassland and fen communities add diversity to the site. The shallow waters contain a diverse fish population, and a wide variety of breeding birds is associated with the mere and adjoining wetland.

THE WASH ESTUARY, LINCOLNSHIRE

Some 66,000 hectares of The Wash Estuary (of which 10,000 hectares are The Wash NNR),
with its vast expanse of intertidal mud flats and salt marsh, is of international importance for its wildfowl.

STIPERSTONES, SHROPSHIRE

A summit rockscape signals the geological importance of this moorland reserve, whose heathland vegetation
varies from high altitude upland heath to more typically lowland heath communities on the lower slopes (above).
Rising high above the upper River Severn valley, the tors, stone circles and stone stripes on the ridge of the Stiperstones
quartzite are an excellent array of frost-shattered and frost-sorted features formed under glacial conditions (opposite).

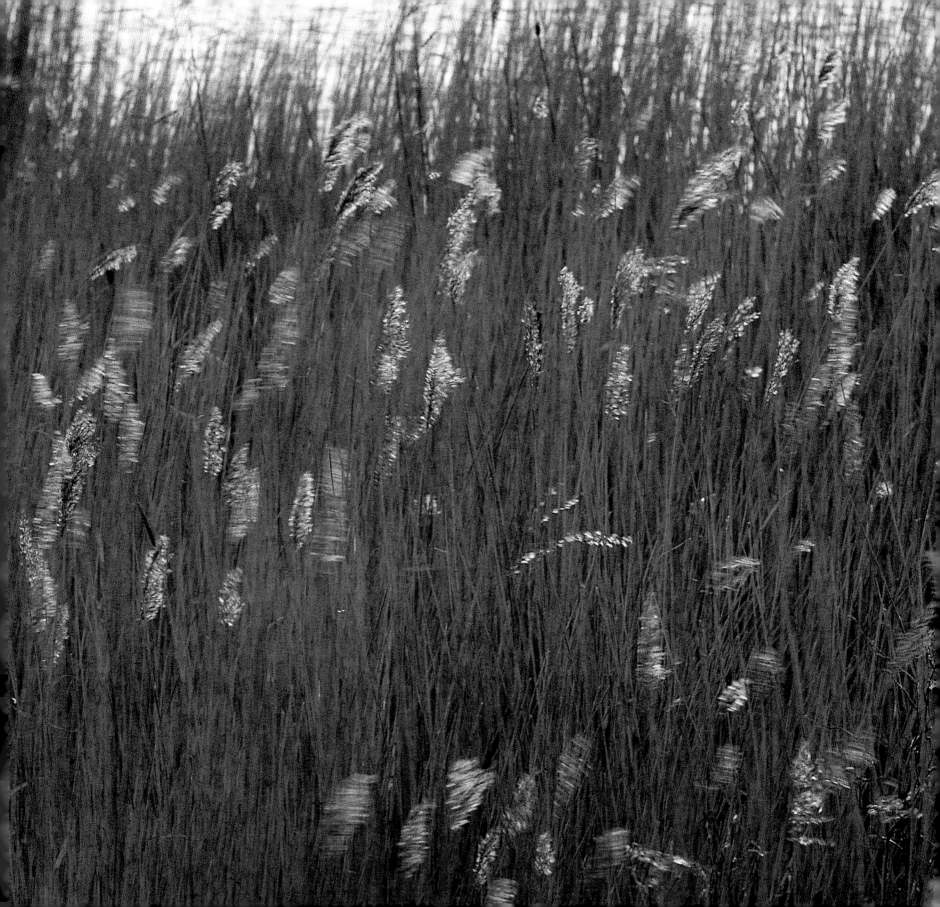

CHAPTER FOUR

EAST ANGLIA

WIDE SKIES AND flat landscapes of grain fields or reedbeds probably typify most people's view of East Anglia. However there is more to this distinctive part of England than that.

The sea, the Ice Ages and man have moulded North Norfolk into an area important for its wildlife and geology. The North Norfolk coast is one of the finest natural coastlines in Britain. To the south is Breckland, a low plateau best known for its heather and grass heaths and home to famously rare birds such as the stone curlew and woodlark.

The reed-fringed rivers of the Broads, which form an important part of a series of wetlands, important throughout Europe, are a magnet to thousands of holidaymakers. The Fens, now well drained, are intensively farmed but still retain a range of habitats including washlands – grasslands deliberately flooded to stop rivers over-topping – open water and broadleaved woodlands.

Over half of East Anglia consists of the East Anglia Plain which is dissected by streams and river valleys. Northwards, there are few hedges and trees, resulting in a fairly bleak landscape. However, in the south, hedges and isolated trees contribute to a wooded feel.

Oh yes. There is more to East Anglia...

HICKLING BROAD, NORFOLK (OPPOSITE), BLACKWATER ESTUARY, ESSEX (ABOVE).

SCOLT HEAD ISLAND, NORFOLK

The prime example of an offshore barrier island in the UK is steadily growing in a westward direction through natural coastal processes. The shingle beaches provide a nesting habitat for three species of tern.

SCOLT HEAD ISLAND, EAST ANGLIA

A ringed plover elevates the practice of nest building almost to an art form.

HOLKHAM, NORFOLK

The many habitats at Holkham NNR include substantial sand flats and sand dunes, the oldest of which contain planted pine and mixed woodland. The reserve also has large areas of salt marsh and wet grazing marsh, and holds an outstanding variety of breeding birds and large numbers of wintering ducks and geese. Dune slacks support the rare natterjack toad.

CASTOR HANGLANDS, CAMBRIDGESHIRE
Small, intimate ponds are one of the rich wildlife features on this mixed habitat reserve. The main habitats are mixed broad-leaved woodland, scrub, and calcareous and neutral grasslands. These mixed habitats often contain a very wide range of plant and animal species, particularly where one habitat merges into another. The reserve also demonstrates the importance of scrub (for nightingales and the black hairstreak butterfly for example) as a habitat in its own right.

CAVENHAM HEATH, SUFFOLK

One of the few remaining Breckland heaths in good condition,
Cavenham Heath also contains damper habitats adjacent to the River Lark,
making it the most diverse of the Breckland heaths. Restoration of arable
land back to grass heath has been successful on this reserve.

WOODWALTON FEN, CAMBRIDGESHIRE

Created in the 1980s, Gordon's Mere adds yet more variety to this diverse reserve that is rich in
plants, insects and birds. The reserve is also home to a wild population of the exotic Chinese water deer.

HICKLING BROAD, NORFOLK

The shallow water and the surrounding reedbeds and grazing marsh support important plants, birds and insects, including the swallowtail butterfly, reintroduced to the Norfolk Broads and Wicken Fen NNR in Cambridgeshire.

HICKLING BROAD, NORFOLK

Norfolk reed is still harvested to provide roof-thatching material.
This prevents a build-up of a layer of dead vegetation in the reedbeds, which keeps
them in a suitable condition for some rare and uncommon plants and birds.

BLACKWATER ESTUARY, ESSEX

Vast expanses of mud flats and saltings, Gore Saltings can sometimes seem of little
wildlife value to the casual observer (above). Tollesbury Fleet, is a place where people can enjoy
and use coastal waters for recreation without significant disturbance to wildlife (opposite).

CHAPTER FIVE

THE SOUTH-EAST

THE SOUTH-EAST is a region of sharp contrasts where dense urban populations are concentrated in and around the major conurbations, particularly London. In the west is the New Forest, then there are the North, South and Hampshire Downs, the London Basin and the Weald.

The New Forest is shaped by its historic common grazing system, with ancient rights and laws. This heathland, mire and pasture woodland is a unique landscape. The Hampshire Downs are open rolling country, their gently undulating plateaux cut by valleys, ridges and scarps. The Hampshire chalk rivers have a clarity and richness that is cherished and revered by anglers from all over the world.

The London Basin is dominated by the capital and characterised by all the effects of urbanisation. Yet it still has extensive areas of ancient and semi-natural woodland including important ancient parkland, for example Burnham Beeches and Windsor Forest.

The North and South Downs seem to mirror each other. To the south, hill-forts and Roman and Saxon remains show early domesticity. Northwards, the light soils were cleared early in prehistory. Between them lie the forested ridges and valleys of the Weald.

DUNGENESS, KENT (OPPOSITE). KINGSTON GREAT COMMON, HAMPSHIRE (ABOVE).

OLD WINCHESTER HILL, HAMPSHIRE

The ancient hill-fort of Old Winchester Hill encapsulates the range of habitats and wildlife features now rare, but once common along the South Downs. Careful management by grazing is required to prevent the woodland and scrub invading the flower-rich open downland.

LEWES DOWNS, EAST SUSSEX

The reserve consists of a hill and a deep valley with steep slopes and varying aspects. The southerly aspect is unusual within the South Downs area and allows plants of a southern oceanic distribution to thrive. These include round-headed rampion, chalk milkwort and kidney vetch. As with numerous other NNRs in England, Lewes Downs is of archaeological importance, in this case for the 'Caburn' Bronze-Age hill-fort Scheduled Ancient Monument.

DUNGENESS, KENT

The largest shingle beach in Britain, Dungeness contains possibly the best and most extensive shingle-ridge flora in Europe. On that part which forms Dungeness NNR, acid heath or prostrate scrub has developed on the shingle ridges, which in turn support rich lichen, moss and liverwort communities. Many rare and uncommon plants and animals adapted to this harsh environment also occur. Open water lagoons are of considerable ornithological importance, particularly for birds on migration in spring and autumn.

DUNGENESS, KENT

Wildlife and low-key human activity have co-existed on Dungeness for centuries.
Other land-uses outside the reserve have had a more significant and deleterious impact.

NORTH SOLENT, HAMPSHIRE (ABOVE)

Remote coastal areas provide safe havens for nesting gulls and other shore-nesting birds.

BURNHAM BEECHES, BUCKINGHAMSHIRE (OPPOSITE)

Shafts of sunlight break the gloom beneath the dense canopy of beech woodland; ancient trees hark back to wilder times.

CHAPTER SIX

THE SOUTH-WEST

IN THE SOUTH-WEST agriculture is the main land use but there are large centres of population and industry around the major seaports. Through the summer months the region is one of the most popular areas for holiday makers, who are naturally drawn to this countryside because of its natural beauty.

The Cotswolds and the chalklands of Dorset and Wiltshire are dominated by the open spaces of pastoral farming. Dense woods are found in the Forest of Dean, whilst the Mendips is an area of varied hills and escarpments. Elsewhere there are intimate patterns of small fields, hamlets and winding lanes.

To the east there are the, still spectacular, remains of the mighty Dorset Heaths, immortalised as Hardy's Egdon Heath. They hold most of the national population of the smooth snake and sand lizard. Further to the west are the uplands of Dartmoor, Exmoor and the Quantocks. Their unusual and diverse range of species reflects the relative warmth of their climate.

In Cornwall the spectacular and rugged coast has provided the background to many a smuggling tale. The remains of the old mine workings remind us of the once-important mineral extraction industry in this area.

LUNDY, DEVON (OPPOSITE). EAST DARTMOOR WOODS AND HEATHS, DEVON (ABOVE).

SOMERSET LEVELS, SOMERSET

A flat expanse of peatland whose wildlife interest is mostly dependent upon a high summer water table, winter flooding and traditional grazing by livestock. Rare plants, breeding and wintering waders and wildfowl thrive in such a landscape.

SOMERSET LEVELS, SOMERSET

Pollarded willows are a characteristic sight on the Levels.
Because of the scattered nature of the fields that make up the
reserve, effective control of water levels is difficult to achieve.

EAST DARTMOOR WOODS AND HEATHS, DEVON

The woodlands on the reserve are among the best of the western acid oak woodlands in Devon. They lie on steep valley slopes and on areas of plateau between the valleys. This woodland type is rare within Europe, and is probably best represented in the western regions of the UK. The reserve has an exceptional assemblage of Atlantic mosses and liverworts, and rich lichen communities. The abundance of wood-cock nests are a notable feature.

EAST DARTMOOR WOODS AND HEATHS, DEVON

The streams running through the reserve contain brown trout, and a small
number of salmon and sea trout come into the streams in summer. They also support a good
range of dragonflies and damselflies, and the grey wagtail and dipper are also resident.

EBBOR GORGE, SOMERSET

A dramatic wooded gorge on the southern limestone escarpment of the
Mendip Hills. A geological feature of particular importance on this reserve is the
presence of two caves whose floor deposits include bones of Ice Age mammals.

GOLITHA FALLS, CORNWALL

The River Fowey cascades spectacularly through this steep-sided valley gorge woodland. The humid, shady conditions provide a suitable environment for a rich variety of mosses and liverworts. The reserve, though only 18 hectares in extent, has a high recreational value with approximately 30,000 visits per year. Circular routes have been provided to ameliorate the trampling damage that can occur, but the riverside walk and falls are the main objective of 70 per cent of visitors.

THE LIZARD, CORNWALL

Coastal grasslands and heaths of unique botanical interest in Britain,
together with spectacular coastal scenery, make The Lizard an outstanding NNR.

THE LIZARD, CORNWALL

The reserve covers several large areas of The Lizard peninsula. Both dramatic cliffs, and inland heaths and grasslands, are included. A series of igneous and metamorphic rocks, known as The Lizard complex, forms the peninsula. The most important of these botanically is the large area of the otherwise rare serpentine rock whose high content of magnesium is the reason for the unique heathlands of the reserve. There are 29 Scheduled Ancient Monuments on the reserve, the most of any NNR in England.

WISTMAN'S WOOD, DEVON

Gnarled, stunted oaks festooned with mosses and
lichens growing among granite boulders, demonstrate the harsh
climatic conditions, but also the relatively clean air of
this woodland high on the slopes of Dartmoor.

WISTMAN'S WOOD, DEVON

The upland acid grassland slopes surrounding the woodland are littered with granite debris. Areas of
heather and several wet flushes containing typical bog plants add variety to the reserve's wildlife importance.

COTSWOLD COMMONS AND BEECHWOODS, GLOUCESTERSHIRE

Ancient woodlands, such as those on this reserve, are rich in snails, beetles
and other invertebrates for which the continuous availability of habitat is essential.

HIGHBURY WOOD, GLOUCESTERSHIRE

Polypody fern growing on the bank of one of the many ancient trackways which lead through the reserve. The damp shady conditions within high forest woodlands provide a suitable environment for ferns, mosses and liverworts.

LADY PARK WOOD, GLOUCESTERSHIRE

Lady Park Wood NNR is part of a complex of woodlands in the Wye Valley that is considered to be one of the most important areas of ancient woodland in Britain. Lady Park Wood itself has not been managed since the Second World War, and is an important area for research into the effects of a non-intervention (ie letting nature takes its course) approach to wildlife conservation. The main tree species on the reserve is beech, but both species of lime also occur.

LADY PARK WOOD, GLOUCESTERSHIRE

The River Wye, of great importance for its wildlife, runs along the eastern
boundary of the reserve. This conjunction of habitats is of particular importance to the two
rare bat species, the greater and lesser horseshoe bats, that are found in the reserve.

COTSWOLD COMMONS AND BEECHWOODS, GLOUCESTERSHIRE

Classic English woodland, hedgerow and grassland landscape that has been shaped by human
activity over the centuries. Wildlife can be very rich in such areas, given sympathetic land management practices.

COTSWOLD COMMONS AND BEECHWOODS, GLOUCESTERSHIRE
High sunlit canopy above the bare boles of beech trees.
Under this canopy at ground level, however, plants that can survive
in shady conditions, such as bird's nest orchid, are found.

Cotswold Commons and Beechwoods, Gloucestershire

A composite reserve made up of several separate woods that together comprise some of the finest beech woodland in Britain. All of the individual woods have a long history of management for timber production, and in more recent times former areas of coppice have been brought into the high forest timber production management regime. As well as the dominant beech, ash is well represented in the reserve, but oak is rare.

EAST DARTMOOR WOODS AND HEATHS, DEVON

Broad-leaved woodland once covered much of England, but relatively little ancient
woodland now remains. That which does is of high importance for its rich and diverse wildlife.

PEWSEY DOWNS, WILTSHIRE

The steep south-facing scarp of Pewsey Downs with its differing aspects
and soil depths, is one of the finest examples of chalk grassland in England.

THE LIZARD, CORNWALL

The rocks exposed on the coast south of Coverack represent the remains of
a former boundary between the Earth's mantle and the floor of an ancient ocean.

EAST DARTMOOR WOODS AND HEATHS, DEVON

Valley woodlands and open heathland of varying aspects make up this diverse reserve. The recently acquired Trendlebere Down section consists of heathland and mires with plant and animal species characteristic of both upland and lowland heathland.

EAST DARTMOOR WOODS AND HEATHS, DEVON

High elevation acid woodland with a ground layer dominated by bilberry,
a dwarf shrub characteristic of woods on acid soils. The acid soils and the relatively
harsh climate substantially suppress the vigour and growth of the oak trees.

EAST DARTMOOR WOODS AND HEATHS, DEVON

Spring flowers, such as bluebells and greater stitchwort, can be abundant in coppiced or open sunny woodlands. The sheltered conditions also provide an environment favoured by numerous butterflies and other insects that make the woodlands hum on a bright summer's day (left). The lower, sheltered slopes of the open heathland are also important for butterflies, particularly high brown fritillary (for which areas of bracken are important) pearl-bordered fritillary and grayling (right).

ENGLISH NATURE

CONSERVING NATURE is essential for creating a good environment. A healthy environment provides the foundation which allows us to enjoy our social and economic prosperity. Where we live. How we work. How we handle everyday life.

However nature cannot hope to survive the pressures of today's society without our help. We must act to conserve its variety and richness.

English Nature is the statutory service responsible for looking after England's variety of wild plants and animals – the country's biodiversity – and its geological interest.

Created in 1990 and funded by the Government, English Nature works with and through other people and organisations – in partnerships. These enable more people to become involved in nature conservation and help them to better appreciate wildlife.

Because wildlife does not recognise man-made boundaries, English Nature looks at the countryside as a patchwork of Natural Areas. Each Area's combination of geology, landforms, land uses and wildlife makes it different from its neighbours.

Using Natural Areas the best of nature can be conserved locally and will contribute to improving what is important nationally.

English Nature does this in many ways. One is to notify outstanding areas as Sites of Special Scientific Interest, or declaring them National Nature Reserves – some of which are featured in this book. These designations provide legal safeguards and English Nature works with the landowners and managers to ensure that the wildlife interest is secure. Outside these areas a wide range of conservation activities are undertaken to make the land, water and sea more hospitable to wildlife.

English Nature's efforts sometimes make the headlines, alerting the public to the disappearance of creatures like the dormouse and red squirrel, and can generate action and support for a range of conservation issues.

Often, however, English Nature's efforts go largely unnoticed as it quietly, but nonetheless actively, works behind the scenes. Government, planning authorities, industry, voluntary groups, farmers, students, amateur naturalists or concerned members of the public turn to English

WORKING TODAY
FOR TOMORROW'S FUTURE

Nature for help and advice on a host of environmental matters relating to the land, sea, and air.

English Nature fully accepts and welcomes the valuable contribution that National Nature Reserves make to the public's enjoyment of the English countryside and the wealth of wildlife to be seen within them. Their policy on public access on those National Nature Reserves that they directly manage is to allow access to the maximum level that is consistent with maintaining the nature conservation importance of each particular reserve. This means that most of them can either be visited at any time, or at certain times through application for a visiting permit. Statutory access along public rights of way is open at all times. Collecting permits are however normally restricted to persons undertaking approved research, or conducting surveys or other study projects.

When visiting an NNR, please observe the Country Code, and in particular do not disturb wildlife or livestock. Remember the principle of quiet enjoyment for all.

Brief details on all National Nature Reserves can be located easily on the Internet via the English Nature website. This includes additional information for about forty 'Spotlight' National Nature Reserves. At these reserves access, including access for less abled visitors, and information which will improve visitors enjoyment and understanding of these reserves is being enhanced. You can find the website at:

http://www.english-nature.org.uk

Information, and visiting and collecting permits, can be obtained from the appropriate English Nature Local Team office, or by contacting English Nature at the following address:

English Nature
Northminster House
Peterborough
England PE1 1UA

Tel: 01733 455000
Fax: 01733 568834

Or you can email your enquiries to:

enquiries@english-nature.org.uk

LIST OF NATIONAL NATURE RESERVES

1 Lindisfarne
2 Farne Islands
3 Newham Bog
4 Kielderhead
5 Kielder Mires
6 Gowk Bank
7 Walton Moss
8 Greenlee Lough
9 Muckle Moss
10 Finglandrigg Moss
11 Drumburgh Moss
12 South Solway Mosses
13 Thornhill Moss
14 High Leys
15 Sandybeck Meadow
16 Bassenthwaite Lake
17 Tarn Moss
18 Cliburn Moss
19 Moor House
20 Upper Teesdale
21 Derwent Gorge & Muggleswick Woods
22 Thrislington Plantation
23 Cassop Vale
24 Castle Eden Dene
25 Durham Coast
26 Teesmouth
27 Asby Scar
28 Smardale Gill
29 Halsenna Moor
30 Blelham Bog
31 North Fen
32 Duddon Mosses
33 Rusland Moss
34 Whitbarrow
35 North Walney
36 Sandscale Haws
37 Roudsea Wood & Mosses
38 Gait Barrows
39 Park Wood
40 Ingleborough
41 Ling Gill

42 Malham Tarn
43 Scoska Wood
44 Duncombe Park
45 Forge Valley Woods
46 Lower Derwent Valley
47 Ribble Estuary
48 Ainsdale Sand Dunes
49 Cabin Hill
50 Rostherne Mere
51 Humberhead Peatlands
52 Spurn Head
53 Saltfleetby-Theddlethorpe Dunes
54 Monk's Dale
55 Cressbrook Dale
56 Lathkill Dale
57 Biggin Dale
58 Long Dale
59 Bardney Limewoods
60 Gibraltar Point
61 Wem Moss
62 Fenn's, Whixall & Bettisfield Mosses
63 Wybunbury Moss
64 Chartley Moss
65 Muston Meadows
66 The Wash
67 Holme Dunes
68 Scolt Head Island
69 Holkham
70 Blakeney
71 Roydon Common
72 Swanton Novers Wood
73 Stiperstones
74 Aqualate Mere
75 Mottey Meadows
76 Collyweston Great Wood & Eastern Hornstocks
77 Barnack Hills & Holes
78 Castor Hanglands
79 Mid-Yare
80 Bure Marshes

81 Ant Broads & Marshes
82 Calthorpe Broad
83 Ludham-Potter Heigham
84 Martham Broad
85 Winterton Dunes
86 Hickling Broad
87 Wren's Nest
88 Sutton Park
89 Monks Wood
90 Holme Fen
91 Woodwalton Fen
92 Upwood Meadows
93 Weeting Heath
94 Brettenham Heath
95 Downton Gorge
96 Wyre Forest
97 Chaddesley Woods
98 Foster's Green Meadows
99 Wicken Fen
100 Chippenham Fen
101 Cavenham Heath
102 Thetford Heath
103 Redgrave & Lopham Fen
104 Benacre
105 Walberswick
106 Westleton Heath
107 Moccas Park
108 The Flits
109 Bredon Hill
110 Buckingham Thick Copse
111 Bradfield Woods
112 Orfordness-Havergate
113 Highbury Wood
114 Lady Park Wood
115 Cotswold Commons & Beechwoods
116 Wychwood
117 King's Wood Heath & Reach
118 Barton Hills

119 Knocking Hoe
120 Hales Wood
121 Hatfield Forest
122 Blackwater Estuary
123 Dengie
124 Colne Estuary
125 Hamford Water
126 North Meadow, Cricklade
127 Chimney Meadows
128 Cothill
129 Aston Rowant
130 The Broxbourne Woods
131 Burnham Beeches
132 Ruislip Woods
133 Leigh
134 Gordano Valley
135 Leigh Woods
136 Pewsey Downs
137 Fyfield Down
138 Ashford Hill
139 Castle Bottom
140 Chobham Common
141 Ashstead Common
142 Swanscombe Skull Site
143 High Halstow
144 Elmley
145 The Swale
146 Blean Woods
147 Stodmarsh
148 Wye
149 Dunkery & Horner Woods
150 Bridgwater Bay
151 Huntspill River
152 Somerset Levels
153 Westhay Moor
154 Rodney Stoke
155 Ebbor Gorge
156 Ham Wall
157 Wylye Down
158 Parsonage Down
159 Thursley

160 Ham Street Woods
161 Lundy
162 Dunsdon Farm
163 Barrington Hill
164 Hardington Moor
165 Hambledon Hill
166 Prescombe Down
167 Martin Down
168 Beacon Hill
169 Old Winchester Hill
170 Ashford Hangers
171 Kingley Vale
172 Castle Hill
173 Lewes Downs
174 Lullington Heath
175 Pevensey Levels
176 Dungeness
177 Black Tor Copse
178 Wistman's Wood
179 East Dartmoor Woods & Heaths
180 Axmouth-Lyme Regis Undercliffs
181 Valley of Stones
182 Hog Cliff
183 Holt Heath
184 Holton Heath
185 Arne
186 Studland Heath
187 Hartland Moor
188 Stoborough Heath
189 Morden Bog
190 Kingston Great Common
191 Newtown Harbour
192 North Solent
193 Titchfield Haven
194 Goss Moor
195 Golitha Falls
196 Dendles Wood
197 Slapton Ley
198 The Lizard

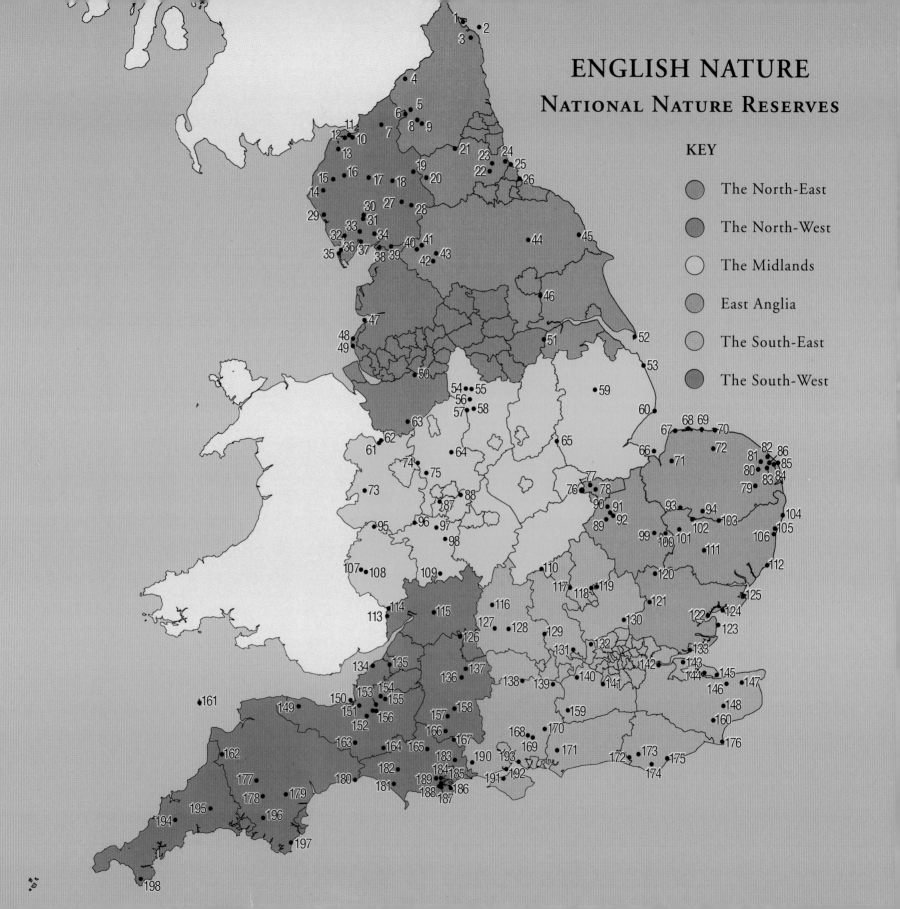

ENGLISH NATURE
NATIONAL NATURE RESERVES

KEY

- The North-East
- The North-West
- The Midlands
- East Anglia
- The South-East
- The South-West

INDEX

Bold denotes photographs